Live Canon
2022 Anthology

First Published in 2022
By Live Canon Ltd
www.livecanon.co.uk

© Live Canon 2022

978-1-909703-91-9

A CIP catalogue record for this book is available from the British Library.

Live Canon
2022 Anthology

The poems in this anthology were longlisted for the
2022 Live Canon International Poetry Prize

Contents

A is for apple

not Adam, said Eve, her
plump fingers reaching out for
the bare red skin of it, blushing
corruption. Like the whole world,
she wanted to hold it in her hands,
to alleviate the tedium, of him
and his rules and reason,
printed on a T-shirt made in
God's image. XXXL.

                         She had
her own shape, wide at the hips
like a ripening pear. From its pips
the apple called to her. To her
fruitier side. It promised a juicier
future. She salivated as thoughts
of puncturing its waxy skin with
her incisors fluttered in her mind.

Adam tut-tutted and talked about
procreation. Eve wanted emotional
and sexual liberation. *A is for
apple*. She held it in her palms
like a final written warning. Then
sunk her teeth in, right to the core.

Natalie Scott

A Trumpeter in Sumy Plays the Ukrainian National Anthem During the Russian Invasion, While in Baltimore, We Hold a Bake Sale

Matt Hohner

At St. Michael the Archangel Ukrainian Catholic Church
they are selling pierogis to raise money for their homeland

not because in a city nicknamed Mobtown we don't know
the recipe for Molotov cocktails, or how to lob them at the

vehicles of occupying forces; not because in a city nicknamed
Bodymore Murdaland we don't know how to kill fellow human

beings in close anger with frequent efficiency, or because we don't
know how to write new anthems for young nations while being

bombed by a despot trying to erase us from the language of maps, but
because sometimes we vogue to Michael Jackson in front of armored

police vehicles manned by uniforms from hostile neighboring counties;
because an old woman in Ukraine walks up to a Russian soldier offering

seeds to fill his pockets so that sunflowers will grow where he falls;
because here, sometimes, a Black man sees a White man struggling to pull

five hundred pounds of mulch to the register at the Home Depot and gives
him a push without exchanging names past thank you, a handshake, a smile;

because we embrace the grace and dignity of freedom exercised in the lunacy
of dancing in front of a line of guns held by men who would rather kill us

than know us; that it's easier to make the everyday heaviness of life collective
than to watch one person struggle with it; that even battlefields will bloom again

where the dead lay now; that small, savory pastries can soothe hearts grieving
for the Old Country, because every mother who has buried a son killed by violence

knows that ache; because we know that sometimes the best weapon against
rocket fire bombardment from a dying empire is to bless the air with music.

Abe

Jill Abram

The mezuzah is still fixed to the doorpost
but he's stopped touching it then kissing
his hand as he enters or leaves his house.
Years have passed since he last walked
across the field and through the village
to shul on a Saturday morning, carrying
his yarmulke and tallis in a velvet bag
and his own siddur, though he can daven
through the entire service without it,
knowing when to stand and when to sit.

He no longer fasts on Yom Kippur
or feasts at Seder; hametz may linger
in kitchen corners during Passover.
His grandmother's silver candlesticks,
shlepped from Lublin over a century ago
lie barren on Friday nights, but at sunset
on 4th Tishrei – sometime in September,
he strikes a match, touches it to a wick
in a potful of wax to burn for 24 hours.
He does not say the Kaddish out loud.

Aisling

Anne Casey

> "And still this life parts your lids, you see
> you seeing your extending hand
> as a falling wave" – Claudia Rankine, *Some years there exists a wanting to escape*

Eyes wide, blazing
hazel against the wild
ochre flame of your hair,
a falling wave—ebbing
of your rebel airs, the rising tide
of your keening

as your fields filled
with the black and fetid—
the bloodied knuckles of desperate
mothers reaping pestilence
from frozen muck to feed
their wailing children,
no crow to shriek
from barren trees.

A scattering of blackbirds now,
raking broken earth, tut-tut at
the ramshackle cart,
a grating lullaby
rising from its
overburdened axles

as it trundles you
towards the waiting
wound, your arm still
extended around your infant son,
bundled with a hundred twiglike others—
today's bitter harvest

to be planted with the rest.

Note: This poem is written in the *Aisling* form and was inspired by 'Sketches in the West of Ireland', an article and illustrations by James Mahoney published in the *Illustrated London News* during the Great Irish Famine on 13 February 1847.

amortisation

Deborah Finding

you explained to me that amortisation
is the depreciation of non-tangible assets
which are things like goodwill and loyalty
and relationships you can depend on

it's a complex calculation, to figure out
what these things are worth, the factors
that add to or detract from their value
and how quickly they can be lost

but I want to try, I always did
I can show my workings out
in your spread sheets, under which
we did, to an advanced level, excel...

I write this as addictive additive, also
when you said you would love me
all of the days. like infinity plus one
but plus one was the problem

which leads us to the minus column
your creative accounting of her
to me, to her of me, every evasion
a reduction of your credit score

and now we disagree on the answer
I show you a number in the red
you tell me of future investments
and paint me a unicorn valuation

but it turns out amortisation is just
the process of slowly writing off a debt
on paper at least, so consider it
done, books balanced, no net gain

loving you was a zero-sum game

An expression of regret

Katriona Campbell

It was all so easy. A few clicks led me
to the garish plastic covers
those jagged
            metal teeth.
The delivery came. I signed my name.
I opened the box and assembled it.
I filled it with oil, adjusted
the tension and fired it up.

Now I see logs and broken
        branches everywhere.
I see sawdust scattered in raindrops and in crumbs
on kitchen counters.
Plates and saucers hold the shadows
        of rings. I can't step into the dining room.

Warnings came from neighbours. Their words echo
through my tinnitus: *Be careful.*
        Of injuries, I thought,
but now I know they meant this loss of innocence.
        I see no way back.

A friend of mine once paid for sex.
        Later, he told me, all his interactions
with women seemed coloured by commodity.
And every time I pass a bush or tree
        I size up its branches
imagine how I'd nestle roaring blades against its base
        feel the tremble of the chain as it melts
        through flowing sap
sense the weight of the trunk as it leans
        towards the cut. Vibrations thrum
                inside my teeth, my muscles harden and I'm pulled back
                inside the living wood the second
                before the snap.

As with sickness
Martyn Crucefix

A breeze blows up as the pressure drops
and there's something wrong
with the steps ahead
though a jaunty tub
of scarlet geraniums
wriggles its flowers to and fro

but start from the top where a few begin
and all the treads and risers
appear level and steady
though if you start
from down below
you'll face instead this lop-sided grin

this prospect of roughened stones
tipped and tilting
beneath dressed slabs
rising straight and apparently true
(yet splashed with lichen
as with sickness—yellow and white—

or is it nothing more than paint
daubed and spilled
by some previous child)
but step if you dare and halfway down
the right side's faulted
if you set out from the top

though if you started from below
you'll catch a glimpse
of sealing cement
on the left dabbed here and there
where warped treads seem
affected by frost or summer rain

though perhaps every riser rakes
left as much as right
to make balance hard
yet some fleeting grace
in having come so far (or is it
the breeze) suggests looking back

your feet at the summit
from where you return
to the garden if you set out from above
then back to where a tub
of scarlet geraniums
has spilled its petals on the ground

Because Simon

Dominic Weston

I will squat outside the door of Victoria Wine until well after closing time
to try and slip a package through its tight-lipped letterbox
because I am that man who buys too much Chilean Merlot from you
and spends too long in your shop buying it

because Simon, I don't know how to talk to you

We only know each other from the shop it's true
I am drinking too much Merlot now it's true
The Diet Coke I buy is for my flatmates, not me, also true

I will discover that the letterbox is a little too narrow for my intentions
and make more than one trip back to the flat to strip them down
because I am that man who puts too much emphasis on these things
and creates elaborate distractions

because Simon, I don't know how to talk to you

You're not desperate enough to go to The Oasis like I do
You don't climb the narrow stairs to Club 49 like I do
You don't even go to the gaily vague Watershed like I do

I will worry that the Police will notice me on my hands and knees
and ask what's in the package hanging on a wire on the other side
because I am a man who finds significance in manufactured symbols
and has made you this anonymised Valentine

because Simon, I don't know how to talk to you

I have cried to Dusty Springfield in Sainsburys for you
I have stolen craft materials from an independent shop for you
I have planned a wedding, even though it's not yet legal, for you

I will wait for a sign now, I will probably wait for a very long time now
and it's pathetic, it's heroic, or somewhere in between
because in six hours or so you'll open up and won't even know it's from me
and write it off as a lame attempt from your ex

because Simon, he didn't know how to talk to you.

17

Bitter from OE biter
Helen Kay

The fox took-away my old hens last night
to feed its starving cubs. Its vampire teeth
parted feathers, pierced the oesophagus
and windpipe below the sinewy neck
and severed the spinal cord, quick as birds
that snatch worms or pluck a butterfly
off a shelf of air. No waste; no signs, bar
sequins of spilt corn on moulted feathers.

Wearing his wife's kimono, a QC, beat
to death a fox caught in the wire fence
round his hen coop, blooded his baseball bat.
I am not bitter, Foxy. The cruellest bite
is the empty plate of death. I would bequeath
you my thighs, breast and legs to plump up
your bony kin. Worse things lurk darkly:
2 million hens gassed and eaten daily.

We will chainsaw the coop, splintering tears
of plywood on the earth. We will plant
egg-smooth bean seeds in our hen manure
and watch the sparrows steal red cherries.
I will stir my tears into a glass of wine
or let them fall to dry on a page of words.
I will wear my fox socks, post #fox pics
cross my fingers, bolt my door at dusk.

Blueprint for Living

Steve Xerri

Welcome to your new home, bespoke
apartment on the bottommost floor
of a self-threading helix plunged deep
into the land, engineered to withstand
burial among clustered depthscrapers,

all vertical corridors and tubes to carry
cables and vacuum-powered lifts. Condensate
traps return breathed moisture to the taps :
our exhaled gases, cooled and chemically
scrubbed, are dispersed in endless cycles

through ceiling vents. You will not miss
the sky : we thrill these days to branching
roots as once we loved the mirrored crowns
of birch and elm trees spread against the blue.
We always were adaptable and now

our children make pets of velvet worms
and sweetly myopic moles. But that's
not the end of it : our waving fingertips
have begun to grow bioluminescent
patches which serve as torches, while

our evolving eyes shine like those of cats
in the low light. Far below Terra's curdled
atmosphere, new world and new body
promise undreamt-of pleasures : loosing
skin from muscle, muscle from bone,

we shuck the shackled flesh, unleash
the immaterial forcefield we enclose
to swim out in fluid earth, released
from circadian solar rhythm, to watch
the tardigrades flock in murmuration.

Celestial

N.J. Hynes

"People's minds need to wander" – Yinka Shonibare, CBE

His new helmet is a bubble filled with sun.
He chose it because it's lighter than any
he's worn before; gloriously warm, it frees
his neck and gives nothing away, this one,
no change in colour to signal a shift in mood
or return to pre-set grey – just silence
and the blue of a cloudless day. More intense
than feel-good pills, plus the euphoria's true.

So why, his brother asks, become the sky?
Why invite others to look through him –
where's his pride? The words beat a hymn
inside his head, slowing his regular stride
but the blue persists, beyond all skin –
he is the sky and the sky holds everything.

Classification of Beasts (subdivision breeding dogs)
Ilse Pedler

after Borges

Limited only by our imaginations let us consider those
who we have blessed with our benevolent attention;

those we have bred for fashion to have no tails
those we have bred for fashion and cut off their tails
those we have bred for fashion to have no hair
those we have bred with blue eyes but cannot hear
those we have bred for fashion and crop their ears
those we have bred with ears so long they drag on the floor
those we have bred for fashion and cannot breathe
those we have bred with shorter jaws and no room for teeth
those we have bred for fashion who struggle to rise
those we have bred with longer spines who become paralysed
those we have bred to have an excess of skin which hangs in folds
those whose skin hangs in folds and develop infections and the itch
those we have bred and killed as their fur goes the wrong way on their backs
those we have bred and killed as they do not have the correct pattern of spots
those who are bred at every season and kept locked in sheds in the dark
those in the dark who use calcium from their bones to make enough milk
those we have bred with their fathers and are born deformed from these liaisons
those who are £50 notes exchanged at motorway service stations
those who whimper when their puppies are taken away
those who are glad when their puppies are taken away
those whose puppies are taken away and whose glands grow hard and tight
and leak tears of milk for absent mouths
those who cower when they hear footsteps approaching because they fear
the hand and the stick held in it
those who cower when they hear footsteps approaching but wag their tails
because surely any touch is better
than no touch at all.

Epitaph for Schools

Sarah Diamond

And so the time came eventually when schools
were bought by real estate developers
when progress inevitably synergized from pedagogy
to economic profitability.
Teachers were retrained in marketing
tactics to ensure client satisfaction
and contracts were short term
based on outcomes from each summer's
data metrics: As /Bs /Cs publicly displayed
on school hall screens and twitter feeds.
Those who fell below their targets were sacked.
Exam boards bought shares in successful
schools and were traded on the stock market
as a bundle called EDUGRO.
Education unions went private
trading their best teachers
under a new scheme : TEACHPRO.
The retirement age was fifty
although most unions expected
their best to last only five to seven years.
Data entry facilitators and TEACHPRO consultants
were recruited from redundant teachers on zero hour contracts.
Schools went global and used
A bespoke software : INSTALEARN
which was selected for its efficiency
and compatibility. Five subjects or *@LearnBots.com*
were offered under the INSTALEARN scheme.
Clients who wished to
achieve *@LearnBots.com* in Literature, Drama, Art or Music
were fortunate to have the *@CultureMeBot.com* option
for two terms. Two terms
were deemed to be the sufficient *@CultureMeBot.com* ratio
of the *@LearnBot.com* curriculum
after the data analysis (trends in career choices
based on university courses offered and accepted)

was carefully scrutinized by the Senior Leaders or SLEDUGROs.
Clients were encouraged to
EDULEARN a carousel of *@LearnBots.com* in NuAge units
Technology NuAge
Genetik Tech NuAge
Business Tech NuAge
and the most valuable of all:
Optimum Interpersonal Strategies NuAge
where the client chooses a brand and an avatar
that best reflects their true selves
for the virtual graduation
ceremony.

Escape plan
Henry St Leger

I am planning our escape. The bank vault in the mayor's
casino basement is due a prison break or two, and so
I'm putting a team together—a hacker, ex-cop, florist,
letter-writer, lion conservationist—to cover all angles.
I have secured the blueprints to the penthouse, hidden
within a larger, less secret penthouse. I have stolen the
heart-shaped key to the safe, and memorized the names
of every pet's birthday. I have bribed the security guard,
who loves it when the naive get together; placed photos
of believable, yet unremarkable crimes over the CCTV
cameras—embezzlement, tax evasion—that society lacks
the political will to actually investigate. We'll crawl
through the ventilation system, doused in factory-scent
cologne, to avoid detection. We'll plummet down the
elevator shaft and remember our training at the last
possible moment. We'll make it out alive and rear
photogenic farm animals on the beach, with new
passports that take a decade off our age, just because.
We'll turn ourselves in, just to dream all over again.

Eventually, Masks Off

Jonathan Greenhause

The sunshine, like Odysseus, returns
to make amends for what seemed several years
of absence soaked in hurricanes & beers
but measure just 12 months. Our spirits yearn

to persevere, to acclimate to Zoom
& other apps that mark how lives can not
just stop: Because if everything we're taught
is fruitless, why not shelter in this room

until we've drowned? Or wallow in regret
like black-veiled widows weeping, begging loss
to multiply? Why scan the seas? Because
each shipwrecked soul deserves a prayer. Forget

this shutdown's sunken fleet, or how your grief's
a bug: You'll see how buds unfurl their leaves.

Eyrar
Laura Theis

on your way to meet a stranger with a dead
phone in your pocket and your unpredictable
shadow in tow with its teeth and opinions you worry
about this impending encounter since your mind is nothing
if not a finely honed anxiety-machine

but as you cross onto the narrow bridgeway
that leads to the open meadow of the nature reserve
you spot her and smile
with the relief of recognition
because she looks just like her online picture

however there is something wrong
with her face
a strange halo of grief
as she gestures to keep you from approaching
you see it a second too late

something terrible to her left
a huge flap of white
streaked with red
it takes your brain
a moment to translate

the wrongness of these colours and shapes
you are seeing into a story
a swan has impaled himself
in two places
on the sharp metal fence

there is something about this scene
that you will never be able to unsee
to find pain where there should be beauty
to go from the moment of not-knowing
to a world that announces time is just code for sorrow

it is like the phone call that one year ago
turned all the people you have left into trapped injured birds
there is something about having to keep
your distance when your impulse is to come closer
to wait with the helpers

but this is a choice you will never be given
still the swan becomes a question binding you to the stranger
on the other side of the bridge and later a lady from the animal rescue
will call you both to let you know that he's eating
that he may make it through the night

falling
Dillon Jaxx

I run into my dad buying oranges at the Co-op / the puckered globes small in his shovel hands as he presses into them with his thumb / *the soft ones are the juiciest* / he tells me every time lifting the citrus to his nose to complete the methodical selection / *mum is at home cleaning* he says laying the oranges in the basket one by one / and he's had coffee with my sister / nobody I knew was doing anything extraordinary that day / except of course somewhere someone was / because somebody always is / I leave the shop holding the orange my dad has gifted me / with his promise of the juicy flesh held within it / ringing in the growing space between us / I feel a chill / a shadow overhead / and lift my face skyward when with a soft bellied thud / a starling lands by my foot / I bend down to check it over / when there is another and another / like an ambush by a soft-shoed army that had lain waiting in the wings / everyone stops / gaping / the street filling in with feathered bodies falling from the sky / tiny red runlets slowly seeping out from under their broken winged bodies / that distinctive petrol puddle shimmer / none of us knew why this was happening / or had any inkling it was going to / as is often the way when the sky starts falling /

For The Bear Spotters

Emma Simon

It's in our blood. Our genes.
That homeopathic trace of long dead ancestors.

The way talk flows as easily
as the second bottle opened on a school night.

How you huddle close to friends, freezing
in your spangly tops, loose-tongued

about who said what, went home with whom,
counting down the hour to the night bus.

No lark full mornings fat with worms for us.
The sunrises we see are heading home,

or bleeding like a headache through a skylight
as sleep at last strong-arms insomnia.

We're the ones who stretch the day
beyond its natural limits. Steal dreaming hours

and fill them with other madcap stuff.
The guitar noodlers, playing a soft refrain,

the yarn spinners and ballad singers,
the one-more-for-the-roaders with their one last tale.

We are the fire keepers, the flame watchers,
listening for footsteps in the dark,

the middle distance gazers, deciphering the shadows
to see which hold teeth and fur.

George
Laurie Bolger

after Morgan Parker

George loves pizza. George stroked a tiger. George likes his girls girlie and will tell you he's tall. George isn't looking for anything serious. George knows this amazing little place by the river. George had his bum out on a cliff once. George. If you like cheese you'll love him. George is a cheeky chappie. George likes his women funny. George usually goes for blondes but George has a thing for brunettes. George will kiss you on the forehead and make sure you get home safe. George doesn't pay rent. George got played on BBC Radio 6 at 4 in the morning. George says fair play. George says his ex was a model. George loves curves, calls you sweet vanilla latte. George's best friend is Nick from the micro-brewery. George paid someone to put together his eco friendly urban wall garden but has a diesel engine. George beckons over the waitress. George calls her honey. George tips her twenty and makes sure you see it. George calls the bouncer buddy. George keeps saying, nice guy. George calls his mummy and you know she won't like you. George's ex sold ice cream from a wheelbarrow. George's ex dressed up like a schoolgirl. George thinks it's sexy when girls read.   George calls the place you were born in a bit of a shit hole. George has so much money. You'd like to take George's money and buy him some socks. George gets cross when they're out of Almond Croissants because he rang ahead and has cycled all the way from Putney. George drives you crazy when you don't hear from him in three weeks even though the last time he drunk dialled you from a Chinese restaurant on The Strand and told you he loved you. George might be dead. George keeps the book of plays you gave him next to his bed. George has a little gold pen with his initials on. George gets back in touch. George insists you meet his parents. George dresses you in his step mum's Barbour coat and calls you a cutie. George's Dad taps your bum at the bar like it's 1950. George says you can really pull that look off   that it's just his Dad's way.

Grief as the Preamble of the Maastricht Treaty
Paul Stephenson

HIS MAJESTY THE KING OF SHOCK,
HER MAJESTY THE QUEEN OF DENIAL,
THE PRESIDENT OF THE FEDERAL REPUBLIC OF REFUSAL,
THE PRESIDENT OF THE PAIN REPUBLIC,
HIS MAJESTY THE KING OF GUILT,
THE PRESIDENT OF THE ANGER REPUBLIC,
THE PRESIDENT OF DEPRESSION,
THE PRESIDENT OF THE UPWARD TURN REPUBLIC,
HIS ROYAL HIGHNESS THE GRAND DUKE OF RECONSTRUCTION,
HER MAJESTY THE QUEEN OF WORKING THROUGH,
THE PRESIDENT OF THE REPUBLIC OF ACCEPTANCE,
HER MAJESTY THE QUEEN OF THE UNITED KINGDOM OF HOPE AND FUTURE,

RESOLVED to mark a new stage in the process living,

RECALLING the historic importance of us,

CONFIRMING their attachment to the principles of love, friendship, and companionship,

DESIRING to deepen the memory of what they shared for a while,

DESIRING to enhance further the functioning of the self in the absence of the other,

RESOLVED to achieve the strengthening and resilience of body and mind,

DETERMINED to promote remembrance, acceptance, and self-forgiveness,

RESOLVED to establish a day-to-day routine as part of coping,

RESOLVED to implement a policy of continuation in order to promote peace of mind, anxiety reduction and sleep,

REAFFIRMING their objective to facilitate the free movement of the individual indoors and out, while ensuring the safety and security of the individual without hijack by sudden emotion or temporary breakdown,

RESOLVED to maintain a close union between the living and the dead, whereby the living is able to make decisions regarding the dead step-by-step in accordance with the principles of time, distance, and incremental progress,

IN VIEW of further steps to be taken to advance individual restoration,

HAVE DECIDED to establish Grief and to this end have designated as their plenipotentiaries:

PAUL STEPHENSON, Minister for Sadness
PAUL STEPHENSON, Minister for Wallowing
PAUL STEPHENSON, Minister for Excessive Drinking
PAUL STEPHENSON, Minister for Sleeping In
PAUL STEPHENSON, Minister for Going Round in Circles
PAUL STEPHENSON, Minister for Replaying the Past
PAUL STEPHENSON, Minister for Regret and If Only
PAUL STEPHENSON, Minister for Old Photos
PAUL STEPHENSON, Minister for Ruminating and Rummaging
PAUL STEPHENSON, Minister for Hoarding and Stuff
PAUL STEPHENSON, Minister for Storage Units
PAUL STEPHENSON, Minister for Not Letting Go or Moving On

WHO, having exchanged their full powers, found in good and due form, have agreed as follows:

TITLE I
COMMON PROVISIONS

Article A

By this Treaty, the High Contracting Parties establish among themselves a Grief Union, hereinafter called 'the Union'. This Treaty marks a new stage in the process of maintaining a close union between the living and the dead with a view to celebrating the past without due hindrance to the present and with a commitment to reconstruction and to the moving forwards towards a future, to be negotiated by the High Contracting Parties.
[truncated].

Her love is a red rose

Arjunan Manuelpillai

I didn't *see it* see it
but I felt it for weeks,

used it to remember
how much I love you.

A woman, full gypsy,
running to a Londis,

a crowd of smoked
bees scrambling into

the cracks between
the buildings.

You just never know
these days do you?

What a man is capable of:
A special brew,

a jugular tonk,
a table leg snapped,

a thousand little shards
falling into line.

There is nothing
we can do but

throw our hands
in our jacket pockets,

shout at a volume
nobody hears

because playing dead
is like romance,

quiet lights, tongues
lowered in reassurance.

The clap of
a shutter down

sets pigeons
into victory salutes.

The woman is
a shook tree

but I do not call
the police.

I'm determined
to make this a love poem.

Now my darling,
I need you to tell me

there is nothing
I could have done.

Hummingbird
Charlotte Ansell

The edges of her seeped out from the mould / the drum she marches to offbeat /
second child trailing trouble in her wake /
the kid who insisted on a cape with her goggles on trips to the pool /
she was always a technicolour
busy busy child /
a flicker flash of brilliance / spark that can't be extinguished /
the baby who chewed up sleep training spat it out /
all heart air brain blur /
whirlwind through the lounge/ leaving a trail of crumbs /
she cannot fuel those wings except with constant snacks /
her knack for collapse /
for lost and broken things / gym kit gifted to the 7am train / 3 pairs of specs already this year /
untold crockery smashed / too many trips to A and E / the way she makes me dizzy /
pacing around me in a circle whenever we have to queue / light as a penny /
a bag of eyes elbows knees fringe / only her Dr Martens to tether her to the ground /
the squirm in front of the TV / I beg her to stop, stay still but she can't /
her answer to everything *wait-what* /
the endless hum of her chatter /
not afraid to square up answer back interrupt / no one wants to be on the wrong side of her tongue /
beloved fierce fearless smart /
her flight path forward backwards upside down /
we don't need answers or solutions or a cure / but she might /
her *trajectory more common in boys* /
pervasive across more than one setting / the *Often* ticks mount up /
her graph plotted on the Conner's form / a mountain range she soars over/
peaks the rest of us could never scale /
she is an iridescence on her day /
we watch her spin swirl fall more often than not /
she is not a diagnosis /
she is magnificent
and ours.

Instagram, will you change my life?

Sana Rao

I left my tea to brew
Too long and now
It's bitter.
What a waste
To throw something
I already have.
I keep drinking.
It is only half-bitter
I could write a novel of things
Half-bitter I have saved when I couldn't
Stomach the whole.
Colonised to believe there is
never enough of everything.
I try to disassemble the bones
That carry Abandoned homes, burnt
Cities, trains piled up with bodies,
A nation splitting in half.
How many somatic healers
Do I follow, to change
The algorithm?

labyrinth

Lesley Sharpe

"The truth is that constancy of a sort is an unescapable virtue; for the things
that the heart is seeking, if they are multiple at all, are very few; they are
found and lost many times over with changing names..." *Freya Stark*

take my hand   the path will not lead us there directly but enter in

unfold your sorrow until it is a spool of thread   a trail behind you

which you will not need when we reach the centre   the way back

is straight and easy   coming out of the heat of things   but you

may not wish to leave   who knows how many times we will enter

follow   find   feel the curve of footpath footfall flesh of thought

that loops back on itself   journeys forth   a dance a dance a dance

aiming for nowhere in particular   finding itself suddenly entering

the pulse of earth that answers back   says   here   here   here

Let's imagine instead

Di Slaney

that you're a man lying here on this couch,
knees wide apart, a bit of flapping paper
halfcovering hope and glory. The nurse
is still a woman, the consultant still a man.
They say how daft you were to have two
operations at the same time, how efficiency
costs in other ways, how brave in hindsight
you must have been, their voices chiming awe.

Let's imagine you've had your left knee done
instead of your shoulder, a keyhole job, far
more painful than you'd thought, nothing
to show but a smidge of mauve around some
invisible mending and your busy knee-man
has already signed you off as fixed. There's
a CD of his expert craft included in his fee,
he likes you to see how good he is, how his

was far the harder task. Let's imagine what's
under this annoying flapping paper isn't
abdominal, hysterohorizontal and zipped,
all the shades of green and brown you never
knew could fill a colour chart – let's imagine
instead that it's throbbing, penivertical and
bunched and scarred and oh so sore so sore
so sore so sore, you can't even bear the weight

of that flapping paper. And as you lie here
with all this aching, stabbing, purpleredness
going on, does your consultant lean in tight
and ask if you've had sex yet? Does he tut
and fingerwag if you say no? Let's imagine
instead that you say yes and wink a grin
as he squeezes *goodman* on your shoulder,
signs off your notes with a huge flourish.

LIFE ON EXO-PLANET GLIESE 433 d

Charles Penty

On the podcast discussion,
a Catholic chaplain
is talking about aliens:

*If spontaneous assembly
into complex molecules
were a property of matter*

*across the entire Universe,
sooner or later
we might encounter*

*beings in need of the Sacraments,
candidates for Baptism
at the very least.*

He turns to the Resurrection –
how 2,000 light years from here,
on some stellar promontory,

Our Lord Jesus's Passion
is only now just happening,
(because all human history

gets transmitted across Space).
Somewhere out there is
a place

29 light years away
that energy from the immense pain
I felt when you died and left me

with its pulse of baleful intensity
(because of the endless time delay)
has still yet to reach.

The planet *Gliese 433 d*,
or the star *Groombridge 1830*
is where I might find a bolt-hole,

(according to the priest's theory),
an elusive quantum particle
of respite from grief.

liplines

Katie Griffiths

> "Prevention – and early treatment – get far better results
> than waiting until they are deep enough to drive through."
> *Sandra Wallace – senior injector**

smoker's lines they say
or kissing lines
her mouth loses track
of what it has birthed

lips that lingered on
the top of a head
still smelling of womb

the woodgrain of her mouth, a pinch of truth

her mouth radiates
the spokes of a wheel
her bike jibbering over cobbles

all the false starts

lips always in danger
lips of the morning fleeing
lips of the evening

a pleated smallholding on her face
her delineated territory
isn't it true that all trails
are breakouts to the wilderness

before guns go off

lips lead the charge
her cupid's cudgel
liplines as tank tracks
the barbed wire she crawls under

cracked earth drawing itself in
a quick dash, her hyphenated self

she gawps like a fish
kissing her mouth in the mirror
luscious lip-pool
gone in unstoppable tributaries

she is running towards the sea
oh let her man those ships

Vertical Upper Lip Lines and Smoker's Lines. Can injections help?
https://cocorubyskin.com.au/blogs/removing-lines-wrinkles-above-lips-smokers-lines-lip-injections/

My Father Retrains as an Interior Designer
Julie Irigaray

1. Burn

When my father retired, he thought his world would collapse
like the roof of a house devastated by a hailstorm.
Divorced and estranged from his daughter, he moved back
to his childhood home to live with his mother.
To avoid her interference, he put his mind to converting
the adjoining farm building into a hideaway
where my grandfather had arranged his workshop. Ten years
after his death, my father finally found the time
to tidy his tools. For four months, he set bonfires on a regular
basis. He burned his school exercise books,
college notes and first job's technical drawings, the blankets
he had nicked from military service, he burned
the sofa from the tiny studio where he'd lived on his own,
crystal glasses and other unused wedding gifts,
he burned all his failures and disillusionments until his
neighbours worried about the thick smoke
emerging from behind his house and called the firemen.

2. Recycle

My father kept one shirt for funerals but gave his blazers,
suit trousers, and Italian leather loafers to the
charity shop. He started wearing his favourite combat
trousers, shabby lumberjack jackets, a thirty
-year-old raincoat and stinking hiking shoes instead.
More for the sake of economy than ecology,
he recycled the farm building's furniture to create an
eclectic patchwork: his parents' 1950s
sideboard with a cracked red marble surfacing, the 70s
grey and brown Formica cupboard where
he stored his hunting belongings, the 90s rustic table
from his first house temporarily stashed
away fifteen years earlier until his wife would get better

and move back with him. Upon discovering
my father's hideaway, I shivered seeing so many relics
of our life together. Now, the three Turkish
carpets from our living-room cover the dusty floor
where cattle used to sleep, my mother's desk
became his, her friend's kitsch floor lamp lights the open
room, and storage boxes with drawings of
my favourite cartoons are filled with my father's admin.

3. Personalise

My father's hideaway wouldn't be photographed for a glossy
English country mag. He decorated the stone
walls of the farm building with a plaster trophy of his first
English setter, sketches of woodcocks offered
to him thirty years earlier, a poster of an old man wearing
a beret with the motto "Hitza Hitz" to remind
himself that the Basques are trustworthy, a picture of him
posing with his long dead dogs for my grandad's
70th birthday. My father managed to create a cosy atmosphere
in a place with no heating and with bats as
co-workers. He uses his phone's 4G instead of a modem
but sometimes needs to sit with his laptop
under the cherry tree to send emails. When I noticed he lifted
the wardrobe on his own to embed it in the wall,
how he meticulously arranged every object (his engineer
attention to detail), I laughed because some
things would never change, and I didn't worry about him anymore.

Night-watchman on the bleach green

Glen Wilson

With eyes accustomed to the dark
I trace the fingers of bleached linen
as they stretch towards the river,

the summer beckoned smell of sour milk
and urine weaves heavy through the dry air.
Distant farmers who have eked out

the last of the light make their way home
for the easiest sleep a man can know,
collies pad at their heels unbidden.

An owl twists her head around,
unafraid to see, compelled to take all
in with her broad binocular eyes.

I count each linen strip, weighted so
the stories spiral on and on, long enough
that a hero can be found a villain

and a love can be a convenience,
or a crutch to make it to the morning,
it's a trove with many imposters.

I spent some mornings with a woman once,
when she was already promised to another,
a fiancé who became a husband.

None of it was foreshadowed, planned,
the both of us just hair pulled with passion
through a hackle of time.

She told me in passing it was done
as if it there was bread on the griddle
that needed her attention.

so now I see purple stains manifest
on these strips of linen each night,
each time wondering if it was a loss

I could have stopped, a dawn
I would have seen if I swivelled
around to see it.

Out of Office

Adrian Buckner

Hawkweeds are not easy to tell apart,
a guide in the back pocket is useful.

Is that campion red
or a hybrid of the nearby white?

I'm sure the creeping thistle
is a little later than the musk.

What is the difference between a nattered
rumour by the re-cycling bin

and a fresh heads-up
on the scree slopes of the meeting?

Is that lush new plan
gasping on the wasteland of your desk?

Don't worry, feathery delights
lounge in the roughest grass.

Will the mould in the coffee cup
bloom in lonely triumph?

Will cress and pink blushed yarrow
enchant our eyes at last,

seed new lanes
and corridors in our minds?

Poem for Frank O'Hara

Antony Mair

Frank, that buggy on Fire Island
came hurtling from the dark as fast
as a hoodlum's fist – no time
to be scared, the dancebar music
still in your ears, and perhaps,
as you wait for the cab they called,
you're thinking of a poem
with Chinese fortunetellers in,
storks and garbage men
and saxophones or perhaps
that blond guy in the bar
who gave you the eye – help me bring
excitement into this poem like a
juggler, say, a dancing elephant
or even you, crashing through
my double glazing this summer night
and asking for a cocktail –
a Manhattan or Negroni –
before you take me in your arms
like you took that blond guy
and carry on as if the buggy
had been a passing seagull
or a dog that cocked its leg
rather than a bolt of lightning
aimed at you by some malicious god—
but would your visit be followed
by a life of bliss in your apartment
or would you pat my cheek
in your usual charming way
then leave to join the waiting cab
and the friends I'd never meet,
the night breeze ruffling your shirt,
without seeing the buggy that will put
an end to all of this –
the parrots, jujubes and the waving palms?

Port Mouse

Tessa Foley

From the Saturday boatshow, tugs burling round,
She's come to our city marquee
a daffydilf bunch in her hand,
Her red, spotty snotrag draped over her shoulder,
it's 9.45 and all signs point to dick,
She thrills every tick from Robert Powell's clinging face.

Schleps from the wasteground, the sewage pontoon,
where the city has edges you can fall off the map,
she crawls through a hole just behind heads,
yanked out into the sun by the whiff of cream cheese,
She's been gnawing on beans up until you chaps,
A guest so green-stupid, she froths at the estuary —

claps at cathedral on her bumpkinish trots,
She is moved by the massive, frenchied by the buzz,
and is shot in both arms by sharp city sounds,
on this ground where there's flavour and v. little taste,
She don't see the smudges like sophisticates can,
not a man just a kid and poor like a skate,

Scrabblin' at slates on the roof of the world,
Jawline to skyline, she guzzles it in,
She's not in with the beings, the complex and smart,
she's hopped into a handcart to swing with the spirals
and paddle with sharks who don't nibble port mice,
Be nice to small fishee, this hum drummer from south,

When she comes to your house, don't shame her
with forks, she can talk like a real'un if you keep her time brief,
but underneath she's the sort who still rifles her coat
when a boy with a sleeping bag asks her for change,
when she turns, walks away, you swap meaningful rolls,
Permanent Landan has worldwised your souls.

There's a break in the sentence once the t-bomb's deployed,
you call her tourishty, take her by the wristy and
show her the skids, put the lid on the city, try squeezing her sour,
But she hears the hour marked by Bejamin's bong,
And she's gone, back to letting the town steal her pants,
You're smug and tone deaf while she still hears the jazz.

Powering
Jacqueline Schaalje

This is the only power you hold onto,
ripped from the dreams none of you believe
are worth the telling. — Rita Dove

Fear is a relative blank until the dogs bark.
The chain stretches out and out, steel scatters.

Mastiff in an open throat, a radius that taps rhythm
of the playfield ascertaining ownership.

I can do this, show me the way to the worry
but I won't go in until the middle.

A passage of fear that doesn't make it better,
not like repeating usually yields a fixing.

Nor does growing up spoil me for this
ragged face, frazzled flight, escholtzia.

A path silking with spring flowers
but that growl is a brown weight.

Now we are face to face, dog to my snout.
I think of a friend's father wheeled from his house.

I carry my own channel around me
but it's silent now. Protection of well-being, can be torn.

This is my house, the mastiff avers.
He is fawn, I am fawn too, but not practicing.

Now I know why I need to keep walking.
Overmuch loyalty is the risk I can't avoid.

Seven Stages of Dad
Jenny Mitchell

Beginning with his death will make this safe,
that's what I tell the page, knowing I can't stop,
even if he rises from the ground, resurrects
his bulk on every line, fists clenched, lips
clamped until he shouts, *You must not speak!*
Those were the words he hurled at me.

Not that he ever spoke that much to me,
huddled in a corner of my body. I felt safe
towards the end, him struggling to speak,
cancer deep inside his throat, a harsh full stop
placed on his right to shout. In dreams, his lips
move fast – *I have the strength to resurrect.*

Why not? He acted like a god – they resurrect,
death a minor obstacle. I know he'd knocked me
down to hear these words, smother with his lips
pressed into mine, used like a wife. Not safe
to tell you more – details may cause alarm. I'll stop
at this – his zip undone, hand on my arm. *Don't speak.*

As if I have the words for what's unspeakable,
me crushed beneath his weight each time he resurrects,
an ache shoved deep inside my back. It only stops
if I cry out, *It hurts too much!* My God, he's haunting me,
crawling under skin, whispering in veins, *Not safe
to tell a word of this*, although words burn my lips.

Standing near his coffin was the same. My lips
felt hot, blistered every time I tried to speak,
say dirt must hold him down to keep me safe,
in the hope that he – a devil – could not resurrect,
walk on holy ground. Still, he feels so close to me,
his voice held in the graveyard trees. *Stop!*

That word lands with autumnal leaves. *Stop!*
It rises up, a bitter breeze that chaffs my lips
as I call out, *He's here!* The mourners stare at me,
pat my arm, say I must not grieve so hard, speak
softly in my ear. They do not see him resurrect,
kick at dirt, a devil's grin to show I am not safe.

He tells me *Stop!* again. Now mourners are not safe.
I yell, *There is no way to silence me! I shall speak.*
Truth falls out of my lips to blight his resurrection.

Sisters

Sarah Westcott

I call up my dead aunt as bird, and we fly
together into velvet non-sense; poured souls.

How easy it is to hitch a bird for flight
and a pretty one too; oh world, we are mere.

I pick up plastic and buy plastic faster than I pick it,
always at one remove. Since I was a baby

I cannot remember wanting anything, until
shame stole in and squeezed my eyes.

I want to say *mother, thank you - you are
the making of me.* I find myself inside

her body again, looking out at the light as she walks
into the garden. *Tell me about your sister*

so I can tell my children, hands in the dust,
earth at her nails, square like mine. *Tell of her*

*smashed spleen, how she could have been saved
if they'd got there quicker, if she'd put a seatbelt on.*

Oh small girls, how far you are,
how far away we grow.

Snow

Vanessa Lampert

Just as I start becoming a more decent person
a past unkindness will fall, silent as snow
from the dark, to settle cold on me

like the pink hopscotch grid I recognise
because I chalked it outside the bungalow
of the two little girls, the day they moved in.

We wanted to play but they shook their heads
no, just stood there in matching red dresses
watching us in silence, holding hands

as we made that game seem
more fun than it was, giggling, leaping,
catching each other's eye as if we sisters

loved one other way more than we did.
We never thought to give them
a second chance and by the end of winter

they'd gone because their bungalow
burned down in the snow. The whole street
turned out to see two little girls

silently holding hands, snow
on their shoulders, snow in their hair
while the windows glowed fierce orange

and cracked. No one cried, no one spoke,
and dirty smoke parted the falling snow
like it knew where it was going.

Successful Communes

Erica Jane Morris

You Tread on my Dreams

Nora Nadjarian

I could tell you so much about what happened but,
really, there is just showing not telling in our house and, yes, I
write and sweat a thousand fragments and long lines, being
the poet of the family who collects words like *impecunious*, poor
poet of the family, and *qu'est-ce que tu as,* what do you have
they ask in French when they mean *what's wrong.* If only
I could make sense of what happened. In my
journal I have written: I don't want to have bad dreams.

It keeps coming back like a starving wolf and I
know he's dead but I run away, write about what I have
seen catching up on me and treading on my thoughts spread
out on the floor like printed sheets in disorder and my
cauchemar sounds worse than nightmares or bad dreams.
There is a film unsuitable for girls wearing pink, girls under-
15. Lo-lee-ta and all the filth and tangle of the French in your
lies and a tongue-twister tying my little feet.

Golden shovel:
"But I, being poor, have only my dreams;
I have spread my dreams under your feet…"
W.B. Yeats

The Company of Fools

Rod Whitworth

When I lived in the company of fools
I was not foolish. I was the one who
washed all the pots and wiped down
the tables, shelves and kitchen counters;
put the books back in alphabetical order
of authors or editors; picked up clothes,
washed them, hung them out to dry;
collected dead bottles, draining them
into my own pint pot for consumption
at my leisure; bagged dimps and remains
of joints to recycle in times of need.

Now I'm back with serious citizens
I find I can't be arsed. There is starlight
to be gathered in, and the song of blackbirds.

The Exhibition of Happiness
Kathy Pimlott

In Tranquillity we're told off for the cultural appropriation
of yoga, for the scarring wrought by a western fad for crystals.
A large facsimile of a crystal, internally lit, looks like it's meant

for a school production of Aladdin. In a film, a true wild yogi
sends seismic breaths rolling from chest to belly and back again
set in a frame of accusatory words – colonialism, capitalism,

you get the gist. Next door the atmosphere conjured up
with fabulous hi-def pics of deep and ancient forest is polluted
by bells escaping from the yoga space, soiling the experience

of blessed silence – silence as in the absence of human sounds.
Bird and creature calls, the drip drip of water, shrug and shift
of trees are constituents of silence, but bells are human noise,

also, we're not the only ones who talk. The promised scent?
We stand by what look like likely vents inhaling deeply
but can't tell if this is it or just the smell of rain-damp coats.

A door marked *Exit this way to Joy* leads to a white corridor
and another door marked *Joy Press button on right*. We do.
We are informed that joy involves an element of abandon.

This is what we came for. People leap, caught open-mouthed
in mid-air above the twang of a trampoline or a splash into a pool.
Children are held in the arc of a cartwheel. Is it enough?

It is not enough. Dance film, stills, engravings show collapse,
possession, twitchy fitting. On a screen, for the whole of *Smile*
as sung by lovely Nat King Cole, a man maintains a smile shape

grimace, gurn, to demonstrate its emptiness and all the while
Nat romances us to smile though our hearts are aching. We do.
Then there's community, joy in community. A bunch of folk,

maybe from the back offices, have been dragooned by the artist into marching round about the Euston Road and Senate House, with empty placards, no demands, having a good time being art.

I am lost. Extracts of texts tease with research into dopamine, the firing up of centres in the brain, haptic responses. Perhaps fifty per cent of us are wearing masks. Something has gone awry.

At the end there's a vox pop, visualised on the wall: what joy is, what happiness means: chocolate, nature, laughing babies, sea. We've seen it all. We're done. Using the app, I input 'sleep'.

The Experiments

Isabella Mead

Somewhere in a lab on the coast
scientists are ogling an aquarium,
breath-misting the glass of their saltwater nursery

through barnacles, sea-urchins and anemones,
where fishing-lines sway slowly
dangling Lego bricks at their tips:

beribboned and suspended, little gifts
bright and defiant and out of context
like pixels onscreen or boiled sweets.

The experiment: to reseed an entire coral reef
brick by brick, for fragile polyps
to embed into blocks of red and green

and this is valid, this is enough:
that, unclipped and set in the ocean,
tentacles will stretch and flourish, unfurl

a glorious fluorescent ecosystem
of limpid oranges and reds and pinks
burgeoning and vivid and affirmative,

replenishing the half-hearted wavering
of its shrunken former self, the ghostly pale
bleaching and retreat, as the womb feels

on dragging days when dull tendrils clutch
at nothing, stirring and rising and shrugging
inside the figure sat staring at a petri dish.

The experiment: for two disparate sediments
to swim microdroplets and mineral oil
and interlock and form a tiny soul,

to flourish and fast-forward to a softly-lit playroom
where Lego pieces lie on the floor abandoned
after hours of being robots and flowers and cars,

and this, too, is valid, this is enough:
that veins are running with a red-brick blush,
diminishing the transparency of water and glass.

The Half-A-Crown

John Lancaster

The news delivers the dead like cricket scores, deadpan.
And with no god jumping off a cloud to help or guess
a future, today I crave past truths to ease the dread, am
coop-flown to The Hanging Gate, newsing and joshing
on whatever happened to Pamela Machin when Frank
pronounces: *all memories grow into childhood.* And
right then unbottled this pouring out of a gone world

how Hezekiah Bailey, who wouldn't let a tractor
on his land, had found a fortnight of weather when
he tapped a rising glass and the wireless gave no rain
to begin his scything and till the mowing done, slept
under a hedge bedded in hessian hen corn sacks,
dropping off to nightjars whirring in the wood, of

how he fed from linen bundles and jugs of nettle beer
his children brought then when his sharpening whetstone
clank had frit the larks and peewits, marked their nests
with hawthorn sticks to save them from his blade, of

how he would send the village folk a call for help
with the scorching hay after his wife had lit an apronful
to show it ready. And we came, shoving two oak poles
called stangs under each hubbled ruck, carted them
sedan chair-like to the barn where he'd pikel the piles up
through the pitching hole till dusk then, face to face, gave
me and Frank and Pamela his thanks – and half-a-crown,

his fairness and the coins cupped gently like new-found eggs,
walked slowly home to share – now that needed fragment
of sense to share before being curfewed back to the pen
and *here we are and what the hell are we going to do about it.*

The Last Books

Caroline Hammond

Sometimes if there's no one else to raise her,
books will take a girl and show her how to be,
a world where swings hang in orchards,
Lady Elocutionists take the stage
and troubles can be met with fortitude.
Lucy Maud Montgomery told me this
the night we fixed the library.
They'd hired me when the qualified staff
refused to work nights after the breach
in the corner set aside for Children's Lit
stories leaked out of un-put-away books
and came to life when the lights went out,
bringing their boats and moats and midnight feasts
till every inch of space was gone and those
fearless daughters who wouldn't mix or share,
made war on each other, while I watched,
then tried to clean up once the mayhem died.
Far worse were the nights of hoof beats and roars,
when I was forced to hide under a desk.
In fact, that's where the novelist found me—
I didn't even try to not look sheepish—
just nodded when she said *fetch the last books*
(you know the ones she means— the heroine
grows up, drably, and makes a fitting end.)
And when these books were open on the desk
we saw them, fully moulded now, serene,
mothers, teachers, wives, accomplished and wise.
I listened to the hum of their voices
as they pacified each animal and child,
till, calm restored, they watched themselves
play nicely for a while, then left me there,
feeling like the girl with long red hair
perched on a suitcase at a station,
waiting to crack slates on careless heads.

the motherbear told

Jane Burn

her cub that it was okay to be afraid   anyone seeing the ocean for the first time
is bound to feel a little overwhelmed   *so deep, so damp, so grey, so blue*
their bare feet test the smallest waves   how quickly each print is swallowed
by the sand   motherbear told her cub all that she knew about trees
some proverb about acorns becoming mighty oaks   how sweet
the freshly fallen taste   how the copper swell of a ripe nut beams
from the split in its spiny shell   how they are hidden against hard times
they worried through drifts of leaves, took the best ones home   rubbed
each leaf with crayon and pinned the wall with paper ghosts   motherbear
made a story for each bird that came to the table to eat   how the robin got
its red breast, how sparrows are really wishes in disguise   *go on, my darling*
try   the window became a page, the picture changing somehow every day
motherbear told her cub about rain   they watched the pathway fill
with tiny seas   splashed and laughed   watched their faces bloom
the pools below as rivers carved a wet way through their shining pelts
motherbear held her cubs's paw, palm to sweet and fragile palm
in the middle of their grip a church of air   warm and filled with scents
motherbear said what was kept so tight between their hands would be released
like a butterfly, brought to life inside this touching of their skins   a mite
of air the shape of wings, swallowed by the larger sky living on,
as molecules of breeze and breath   *see that cloud?   well, that will be*
motherbear watched each season wither its own way past   learned the shapes
of winter   how snow is just another word for cold   for something
lying quietly   over everything she knows

The Raft

Chrissy Banks

i

I walk through the door to Maternity –
gladly, nobody makes me.
Now is the time.

Tuned to this sea inside, this ebb and flow,
strange not to know till now
how each time the wave swells,

I can shift my whole self
down, into my birthing muscles, and push.
Then let go, lie back and float.

Soon it gathers again, wave after wave
that builds, falls, lands him at last
onto the drenched beach of my body.

A peal of voices rings out. A flurry of busy hands.
He snuffles and roots. He is home
on my breast, my arms a harbour.

And the warmth of him.
He blinks into the light and I'm dazzled
as if I have swallowed stars.

At night, they take the babies away,
so you can rest. I lie awake, listening.
I know his cry as well as I know my own name.

ii

This is a different country. Empty sand, the ocean
far out. Everyone here is a stranger.

Children ourselves, we take up the props of adults:
two Scandi chairs and a sofa; a bookcase, an abstract print.

He lies statue-still, his breathing so soft
I can never be sure if this is just sleep.

Waking, he howls till I fear he'll hurl
his insides out through his mouth.

Anyone passing could see us, marooned,
missing the beat to each other's language.

But nobody stops and when his father returns each night
he never remembers the lifeboat.

iii

Each day I wash up, make a fire
breaking off when you cry
to gather you in

and you cry so much
your legs scrunched up
in what my body says is pain

and why don't you smile
like other babies   you are supposed
to smile and why don't you sleep

they say I am to blame
your anxious mother
I am the reason you cry

I thought at your birth
mothering would find me
forgive me I will be calm again

iv

love was the raft that kept us afloat
each day I discovered afresh
the sweet warm weight of him

I started to say love was easy
the way it came in flowing like milk -
but no it was never as simple as that

there were days sun slipped
below the horizon   darkness
came down   we were rudderless

a comfort to notice
lights twinkling onshore
the wind blew us towards them

The Snowball of Thanatos

CY Forrest

and, far — the weight, the expectation, the north,
the university, the cancelled train, the backpack full
of text books; to the broken strap, to the late arrival,
to the bored flatmate who watches Hunterwali,
to the sofa, to Fearless Nadia who whips up a storm
in Hindustani. To the emergency news bulletin,
the noise of the new; to speak ill of the language,
of the microwaved dinner, of the ongoing argument,
of the Snowball of Thanatos. To Jo Shapcott:
'language is impossible in a country like this';
for the text books lost, for the deep puddle,
to the Oxford Junior Dictionary, the name of the kingfisher,
the acorn dropped, the buttercup lost, the snow
leopard; to the super-sun, that melts the ice.

The women of 10x3

Alison Binney

Getting you out of hospital is the latest thing
I think I should know how to do, and don't,
but I have Donna's number on a post-it.
I'm not sure who Donna is but when she picks up
and calls me *darling* I nearly cry.
You're not her remit any more, Donna says,
but she hands me over to Hollie
who calls Amber from Respite Care.
Hollie will get you transferred this afternoon
and once you're settled, Keeley and Kayleigh
will be in touch. And now we have a plan,
and I know it will be OK because we both
trust these women with the names of girls
who sat at the backs of our classrooms years ago,
you about to retire, me just starting out,
the ones who'd warn us when a lad farted,
who cared enough to chew without us seeing,
the ones who'd lend a highlighter, and print
coursework in 14 pt with bordered hearts.
Sometimes they'd be off and we'd find out
there was a brother with Down's or a nan
who wanted the company, and it would make sense,
then, that point they'd made about Juliet and the Nurse,
when we'd picked on them one Friday afternoon,
and realised there was more going on.
They're tattooed now, often, which you enjoy,
though you'd never have brooked one on me.
It's something to chat over while they're helping
you on with your socks, the hearts filled
with children's names, the no-good men
morphed into dolphins. They make it all look
as easy as you once made poems seem, or tried to,
these impressive capable Ambers and Dawns
who've learned to read between your lines,
to breathe warmth into the hard words.

And now Hollie with the mermaid tattoo,
coming down the ward with her clipboard,
who will sign your discharge papers
with a circle over the *i,* then follow me out
to ask if you'd like a man to change your pad.

This Is BBC 1, Now the 9 O'clock News

Hilary Watson

Snowy the rabbit is worried about the fox staring at her,
licking his lips in the night, so I need Daddy to read
the next chapter so Paddy can tell Sophie what to do
with the sack. I wish the man could stop talking.
Peter Sisson says children have lost their homes in Kosovo.
Sarah and Kirsty have two horses. Their Bampy
has racer puppies in a cage in his garden.
Auntie Chrissie talks about her older husband,
talks about sex. I laugh like everyone but she looks
at me in the mirror in the car and says 'sometimes
adults do talk about sex, you know.' Her friend
smells like tobacco. He throws his Quavers pack out
the window. Ych-a-fi. We learned that in Welsh.
And mae hi'n bwrw glaw. And ga i fynd i'r ty bach
os gwelwch yn dda to go to the toilet because Mrs Evans
always says yes to that but in English she says no,
she says why didn't you go at playtime? The box of ropes
smells ych-a-fi. I like making bubbles with soap.
The hot tap doesn't work. The paper towels smell blue.
I drew a picture of St Lucia which is an island,
and I got a pen pal called Clara in Prague - which
isn't in Czechoslovakia. I don't know where Kosovo is
and no one gave me an address for any girls there.
When I'm bigger I could go and maybe recognise
the girls and boys from off T.V. The News is always on.
On weekends it's even later. If Daddy read to me instead
we'd have done the scary bit and found the pot of gold.

Visiting Woodhenge and The Church of St Mary and St Melor, Amesbury

Josephine Corcoran

It is the story of a woman
whose understanding travels dreamlike
between two places. One scorching day

she adds her fingerprints
to a stone-and-timber neolithic circle
to an early church.

Time, a dandelion clock.
Knowing, unknowing, she steps
on footprints, belongings, bones,

returning and returning to a mound of flint,
small inhumation, flowers and grasses
shaped like circles, little offerings.

Mary's robes, blue as cloudlessness,
upright baby in her arms, cool stone walls
forgive the heatwave, rows of shining candles.

She has read poems, heard mother
cows outside a slaughterhouse, cried
in cinemas, scenes of small unslept-in beds.

In newspapers, history books, read
of disappearances, violence, children
owned, bartered, sacrificed,

stored all this, her heart an aching place,
plot of ancient pain
where coins are thrown for luck & children

make daisy chains, singing wishes
while parents hold up their phones like lanterns.
No holy water in the font, but gypsophilia.

She dips her hand in baby's breath
also known as maiden's breath,
closes her eyes in sunlight, as if she is half-waking.

White Flag

Mark Fiddes

It was hardly the offensive we expected.
A few marigolds had their necks broken.
Roses that petalled late were detonated
at a safe distance under a hail of conkers.
This morning, swifts wheel homewards
on brand new air that has been chilled
above container seaports west of here.
Still reckless and loose with summer
we go through the usual commotions
that fill our kitchen with vapours.
The holy ghost of slightly burned toast.
An old kettle heaves. Stove eggs rattle.
We sup tea's humble beatitudes.
Somehow the heating has turned itself on
waking flies and a thump in the roof.
The radio flips from Elgar to news of war.
Reporters call it a strategic withdrawal.
Beefy generals, who left their guns behind
in the rush, quote Aristotle and Sun Tzu.
More butter, please, and sweet preserves
prickled from our hedgerows and hearts,
a child's blackberry drawn on the label
and the sticky plates we will never replace
because these are our chipped histories.
This is how we start delicate negotiations
with the sallow envoys of winter.
For we are the meek and the peacemakers.
Ours is the sourdough of Heaven.

Wolf sister, running

Tamsin Hopkins

She would not come away
with me

                              I tried everything
                         lit a fire, told the stories
                         I thought she softened
                    when I spoke of our home
                                        trees, tall
                               in our girlhood

                               but we are both
                                  in snow now

                                    I'd searched
                      frozen tundra by sled
                      my voice a raw thing
                                       calling

                          like a white mirror
                            it rejected me

                                   I stopped,
      dismounted at the slightest shadow, dragging
                 legs through deep snow
                              I searched

                             excavated every
                                      hollow

                              every frozen
                                  leafless
                                      twig

by chance I discovered her spoor

             in a small clearing
sunlight had found her

rock and ice
her only protection

my throat filled, flaked
with white

> At my voice
> eyes slid away

> her head
> was still fine, skin a tight covering
> but her body
> her feet were
> transparent

> I whispered all her names
> *Love, Baby, Pet, Sister, Darling*

> even though she recognised me
> I could not get close

the journey back
  a hurry of breath
every Husky in the team
  a running intention

> I couldn't give her up
> Nor could I keep her

> For a time I was lost
> Daily I twisted a braid from hair I took
> the same colour as my own

the glassblower knew what to do:

                    she burned the last of my sister's hair
                            ash melted, my girl
became crystal

wolf
not lost, she, we, always
running
cold
together,
her claws
marking tracks on ice
the length of my mantlepiece

a glassy snout, a running front paw hovering
as if on snow

Your test kit is in the post

Joolz Sparkes

Q.   A petri dish containing bacteria was found in the colony. Who finalised it?
A.   A wet regime; it's a closed market shop, mind your own business.

Q.   At what point was the alarm raised in the colony when they encountered
     the splitting technique?
A.   Once every inhalation through a handmade cloth mask bought on Etsy.

Q.   When tapping the app later, who was the whistle blower?
A.   The monkey in the lab with half his skull showing.

Q.   If the man has no widow and drinks beer while watching football, could
     he have seen the crisis looming?
A.   Not if he was dead set on going to the pub.

Q.   Will the dish ever be full, or will it always contain a single bacterium?
A.   The doctors cannot agree but you can find the definitive answer in the
     comments section of a tabloid, you bedwetting sheep.

Q.   Can single-use plastic be tossed in the sea from passport freedom
     getaways?
A.   It's your right to leave souvenirs annually; the currency is irrelevant.

Q.   What if the cell divides and the colony is fatally compromised?
A.   Ask the bats for survival technique; pipistrel know the ways of the
     pipette
     and white men only gaslight.

Q.   But will the widow be kind to us once the colony is dead?
A.   She can only have one visitor for half an hour waving through a
     window. Wait your
     turn to be magnified by microscope.

LIVE CANON